The Mac
is not a typewriter
Second Edition

The Mac
is not a typewriter
Second Edition

A style manual for creating
professional-level type
on your Macintosh

Robin Williams

Peachpit Press
Berkeley ▪ California

The Mac is not a typewriter, Second Edition
©2003 by Robin Williams

PEACHPIT PRESS
1249 Eighth Street
Berkeley ▪ California ▪ 94710
800.283.9444
510.524.2178 voice
510.524.2221 fax

Cover design and production: John Tollett
Interior design and production: Robin Williams
Peachpit Press is a division of Pearson Education.

ISBN 0-201-78263-4
10 9 8 7 6 5 4 3 2
Printed and bound in the United States of America

*To **Barbara Sikora**,*
a shining star.
With love,
Robin

About the author

I live and work in Santa Fe, New Mexico. In 1985, after several years of teaching traditional graphic design and typography, I discovered the Macintosh. It didn't take long to switch from t-squares-and-triangles-and-rubber-cement-and-rubylith-all-over-the-place graphics to turn-off-the-switch-and-the-mess-is-all-cleaned-up graphics. I have taught desktop design, electronic typesetting, web design and production, and related technology courses around the country.

I have written many other books, including:

Robin Williams Mac OS X Book, Jaguar edition

The Little Mac Book (eighth edition, Mac OS 9)

The Little Mac iApps Book

The Little iMac Book

The Little iBook Book

How to Boss Your Fonts Around

A Blip in the Continuum

Windows for Mac Users

The Non-Designer's Design Book

The Non-Designer's Type Book

The Non-Designer's Scan and Print Book

The Non-Designer's Web Book

Robin Williams Design Workshop

Robin Williams Web Design Workshop

Robin Williams DVD Design Workshop

Contents.

■

9

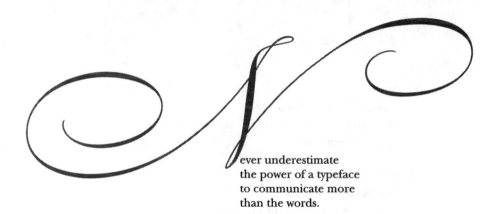

ever underestimate
the power of a typeface
to communicate more
than the words.

— *Robin Williams*

Read me first

There are no little things.

This book first came out when the incredible phenomenon of desktop publishing was just starting to take over the professional typesetting business. But life in the digital lane moves so fast that now there are new generations of designers and computer users who have never even *seen* a typewriter. Today, professional-level type is just a way of life—even the smallest business or the most harried college student can create high-quality pages, from annual reports to a letter to Mom to theses papers to visual presentations.

But whether you've ever used a typewriter or not, those professional typesetters whose jobs we have replaced knew things about type that you might not have been taught. This book does not pretend to be a treatise on design or typography or desktop publishing—there are many excellent books available in those areas. Rather, the purpose of this book is to let you in on some of the basic techniques that have been used for centuries to make type pleasing, beautiful, readable, legible, and artistic.

Many of the concepts presented in this book are subtle, yes—but they add up to a professional look. Perhaps most people couldn't put a finger on exactly what *gives* it that look, but everyone is aware of it. Since we snatched type out of the hands of professionals, then we must upgrade *our* awareness of what made their work *look* professional. It's simply a matter of raising our consciousness, of looking closer at our printed pages with a more critical eye.

The Mac is not a typewriter. Yes, the title of this book is getting old-fashioned, but the concept is the same. The type we are using is not mono-spaced, mono-weight, mono-sized, mono-boring; it's capable of being the highest quality.

I strongly feel it is our obligation—every one of us who uses the computer to create text on a page—to uphold the highest possible level of typographic quality in this changing world.

■

What about the web?

Most of the principles in this book apply to printed pages, not to the default text on web sites (text that is created as a graphic, however, should follow all the guidelines in this book). See Chapter 21 for the typographic techniques that we have to let slide on the web—for now, anyway. The future is on its way.

One space between sentences

Use only one space after periods, colons, exclamation points, question marks, quotation marks—any punctuation that separates two sentences.

"What?" you say! Yes—for years you may have been told to hit two spaces after periods, and on typewriters (if you remember those) you should. But your Mac is not a typewriter.

On a typewriter, all characters are **monospaced**; that is, each letter takes up the same amount of space—the letter **i** takes up as much space as the letter **m,** and a period (.) takes up the same amount of space as a capital **W.** Because all characters are monospaced, the tradition was to type two spaces after periods to separate sentences.

But most of the fonts you'll use on your Mac are **proportional**; that is, the characters each take up a proportional amount of space—a typical letter **i** takes up about one-fifth the space of the letter **m.** So you no longer need extra spaces to separate the sentences. Take a careful look at these two examples:

```
Notice in this paragraph how the letters
line up in columns, one under the other,
just as on your typewriter.  You could
draw vertical lines between the columns
of letters.  This is because each
character takes up an equal amount of
space.  This monospacing is what made it
desirable to use two spaces to separate
sentences on typewriters.
```

This paragraph, however, uses a font with *proportional* spacing. Each character takes up a proportional amount of the space available. Thus the single space between sentences is enough to visually separate them, and two spaces creates a disturbing gap.

> This paragraph uses a proportional font. I have set two spaces after each period. Squint your eyes at this text. You'll notice what big gaps those extra spaces create. I guarantee this: never in your life have you read professionally set text printed since 1942 that used two spaces after each period.

Of course, this one-space rule applies just as well to the spacing after colons, semi-colons, question marks, quotation marks, exclamation points, or any other punctuation you can think of. Yes, this is a difficult habit to break, but it must be done.

Pull down any book on your shelf—you won't find two spaces between sentences (the only exception will be publications or advertisements produced on a personal computer by someone who was still following typewriter rules). Your eye does *not* need that extra space to tell you when the next sentence begins.

If you don't believe me, check with the goddesses of all things editorial: *The Chicago Manual of Style*. You'll find answers to lots of questions at: www.press.uChicago.edu/Misc/Chicago/cmosfaq

Now, you might be working for someone who *insists* there *must* be two spaces after periods. If it's not going into your portfolio, it's not worth fighting about. If that person insists their printed pieces should look amateurish, unsophisticated, and unprofessional, so be it.

In papers you turn in for school where the instructor insists on two spaces, use two. In unpublished papers, email, personal correspondence, use as many spaces as you feel comfortable with. But once it gets to press, don't make yourself look foolish.

On your Macintosh, the fonts Monaco and Courier are monospaced, just like most typewriter fonts. These fonts are sometimes required for special purposes, like in screenwriting, or perhaps your editor insists that your manuscript be set in Courier. As always in special circumstances, follow the guidelines set for that particular field.

Quotation marks

*Use real quotation marks—never those grotesque
generic marks that actually symbolize ditto marks:
use " and " — not " and ".*

Of course, on a typewriter (if you've ever used one) when you wanted
quotation marks you used the typewriter quote marks, the ones that
otherwise one would think are ditto marks or inch marks (") and
foot marks ('). Those symbols are never found, though, as quotation
marks in a book, magazine, ad, poster, etc., simply because that is not
what they are.

Fortunately, the Mac provides us with real quotation marks.
Unfortunately, they're tucked away on one of those invisible keyboards
that you can only see with the Key Caps utility (see page 25 for more
info on Key Caps). It takes an extra second to access the true quotes,
but you get used to it. The added professionalism they give your work
is very well worth the effort. This is where they are hidden:

Opening double quote:	"	*type:* Option [
Closing double quote:	"	*type:* Option Shift [
Opening single quote:	'	*type:* Option]
Closing single quote:	'	*type:* Option Shift]

Do you see the pattern? When you are typing, instead of hitting the "
key, hold down the Option and/or Shift keys together, and then tap
the opening or closing bracket (near the Return key). You may even
want to put a piece of tape on those bracket keys and draw in the
proper quote marks to remind you exactly where they are.

Most software applications will convert the typewriter quotes to the
real quotes for you automatically as you type. Check the preferences
for your application—you'll find a checkbox to tell your application

■

to automatically set something like "typographer's quotes," "smart quotes," or "curly quotes." Then as you type using the standard ditto key ("), the software will set the correct quotation marks for you.

But it is necessary to know how to set them yourself because **sometimes the software does it wrong.** For instance, your application turns a generic " into an opening or a closing quote depending on whether there is a space in front of the character or not. If you type a sentence like the example below, the quotation mark will automatically go the wrong direction (because there is no space in front of it) and you'll need to manually replace the mark. Also see the examples on the opposite page for more reasons to know how to set quotation marks manually.

> **As she wrapped him in an enigma—"Help, help, he cried"—she laughed maniacally.**

Correct quotation marks are also available at your Desktop when you're naming files, as well as in the Save As dialog boxes, in paint programs, database and spreadsheet programs—anywhere you can type. There's no excuse for not using them.

> **Typewriter quotation marks are the single most visible sign of unprofessional type.**

My rant: *It absolutely astounds me that in the 21ˢᵗ century there are people getting paid lots of money to create huge Hollywood posters, expensive television commercials, slick magazine ads, and DVD menus who don't know how to set apostrophes and quotation marks. What schools did they go to? Who taught them? Who hired someone who doesn't even know how to set an apostrophe? Sheesh.*

■

Avoid this foolish mistake!

If you let your software create the apostrophes and quotation marks for you without being aware of what they are supposed to look like, you might end up with embarrassing results like these (which I have actually seen so many times):

Bridge Clearance: 16' 7"

The young man stood 6' 2".

The length of the wall is 153' 9".

Of course, these should really read:

Bridge Clearance: 16' 7"

The young man stood 6' 2".

The length of the wall is 153' 9".

*The periods are on the outside of these marks because they are **not** quotation marks—they are inch marks and so are treated like any other character.*

Technically, *inch and foot marks are called "prime" marks, and they are slightly slanted. In the examples above, I used the typewriter quotation and apostrophe marks and made them italic so they would look proper. A few fonts, like the Symbol font and some high-end OpenType fonts, include prime marks.*

Punctuation used with quotation marks

There often seems to be confusion about where quotation marks belong when there is punctuation involved. These are the rules:

- In America, commas and periods are **always** placed **inside** the quotation marks. Always. Really.

  I thought to myself, "Your attitude is your life, Robin," and realized it's true.

  The title of the essay is "Not for the Slow-Headed."

  Her motto was always, "Go singing through the world."

- Colons and semicolons go **outside** the quotation marks.

  The name of John's DVD business is "Thunder on the Left"; when you hear thunder on your left, it means the gods have a message for you.

  Then there's her phrase, "Upcheer thyself": it's a plaintive wish in light of what happened later.

- Question marks and exclamation points go **in or out**, depending on whether they belong to the material inside the quote or not. Logically, if they *belong* to the quoted material, they go *inside* the quote marks, and vice versa.

  She cried, "What a time to be me!"

  Can you believe he claimed, "I work hard"?

- If more than one paragraph is quoted, the double quote is placed at the *beginning of each paragraph,* but only at the *end* of the *last one.* What an interesting convention.

postrophes

Use real apostrophes, not the foot marks: ' not ' .

This is actually exactly the same as the previous chapter, but I set it off separately because it is so important, and often people don't connect quotation marks with apostrophes. But the apostrophe is nothing more than the single closing quotation mark.

Repeated from the previous page:

> *Apostrophe:* ❜ *type:* Option Shift]

Apostrophe rules

Many people are often confused about where the apostrophe belongs. There are several rules that work very well:

For possessives

Turn the phrase around. The apostrophe will be placed after whatever word you end up with.

For example, in the phrase **the boys' camp,** to know where to place the apostrophe say to yourself, "The camp belongs to the **boys.**"

The phrase **the boy's camp** means, "The camp belongs to the **boy.**"

Another example: **the women's room** means, "The room belongs to the **women.**"

> #### The big exception is "its."
> "Its" used as a possessive *never* has an apostrophe!!! The word **it** only has an apostrophe as a contraction— **it's** always means "it is" or "it has." **Always.**
>
> When you read **it's,** say to yourself, "it is."
>
> The pronouns **yours, hers,** and **his** don't use apostrophes—and neither does **its.**

■

For contractions

The apostrophe replaces the missing letter. Simple rule.

For example: **you're** always means **you are;** the apostrophe is replacing the **a** from **are.** That's an easy way to distinguish it from **your** as in **your** house and to make sure you *don't* type: Your going to the store.

As previously noted, **it's** means "it is"; the apostrophe is indicating where the **i** is left out. **Don't** means "do not"; the apostrophe is indicating where the **o** is left out.

For omission of letters

The apostrophe replaces the missing letter. Simple rule.

In a phrase such as **Gone Fishin',** the **g** is missing.

In a phrase such as **Rock 'n' Roll,** there should be an apostrophe *before and after* the **n,** because the **a** and the **d** are both left out.

And don't turn the first apostrophe around—just because it appears in *front* of the letter does not mean you should use the opposite single quote. An apostrophe is still the appropriate mark (*not* **'n'**).

In a phrase such as **House o' Fashion,** the apostrophe takes the place of the **f.** There is no earthly reason for an apostrophe to be set *before* the **o.**

> This is WRONG: **Band 'o' Brothers**
>
> This is WRONG: **Band 'o' Brothers**
>
> This is CORRECT: **Band o' Brothers**

To distinguish decades, temperature, and ages

In a date when part of the year is left out, an apostrophe needs to indicate the missing year. **In the '80s** would mean the decade; the "19" is left out. **In the 80s** would mean the temperature.

Notice there is no apostrophe before the **s**! *Why would there be?* It is not possessive, nor is it a contraction—it is simply a plural. For instance, if someone is **in her 80s,** she is growing older; 80s is plural.

ashes

Never use two hyphens instead of a dash.
Use hyphens, en dashes, and em dashes appropriately.

Everyone knows what a hyphen is—that tiny little dash that belongs in some words, like mother-in-law, or in phone numbers. It's also used to break a word at the end of a line, of course.

You might have been taught to use a double hyphen to indicate a dash, like so: -- . This is a typewriter convention because typewriters didn't have the real dash used in professional typesetting. On a Mac, no one needs to use the double hyphen—we have a professional **em dash,** the long one, such as you see in this sentence. We also have an **en dash,** which is a little shorter than the em dash.

hyphen	-
en dash	–
em dash	—

See the following pages for details about when to use hyphens and dashes and how to type them.

∎

Hyphen –

A **hyphen** is strictly for hyphenating words or line breaks. Your punctuation style manual, such as *The Chicago Manual of Style,* goes into great detail about the proper use of hyphens.

There doesn't seem to be a lot of confusion about *when* to use a hyphen, especially since your computer automatically inserts them at the ends of lines when necessary. But see Chapter 12 for some guidelines on how to make sure excessive or wrong hyphenations don't make your work look amateurish.

To type a hyphen

> **hyphen** –   Between the zero and the plus sign
> at the top-right of the keyboard

En dash —

An **en dash** is called an en dash because it's approximately the width of a capital letter N in that particular font and size. It is used between words that **indicate a duration,** such as time or months or years. Use it where you might otherwise use the word "to."

In a page layout application, the en dash can be used with a thin space on either side of it if you want a little room, but don't use a full space. (Check your manual for how to set a thin space.)

Here are a few examples of places to use the en dash. Notice that these are really *not* hyphenated words, and a plain hyphen is not the logically correct character to use. Notice that you automatically read the en dash as the word "to."

> **October – December**
>
> **6:30 – 8:45 A.M.**
>
> **4 – 6 years of age**

The en dash is also used when you have a compound adjective and one of the elements is made of two words or a hyphenated word, such as:

> **Santa Fe–Chicago flight**
> *(if you used a hyphen here, you'd be taking the Santa "Fe-Chicago" flight)*
>
> **pre–Gulf War period**
>
> **high-stress–high-energy lifestyle**

To type an en dash

en dash — Option Hyphen
hold the Option key down, then tap the hyphen key

Em dash —

The **em dash** is twice as long as the en dash—it's about the size of a capital letter M in whatever size and typeface you're using at the moment. This dash is often used in place of a colon or parentheses, or it might indicate an abrupt change in thought, or it's used in a spot where a period is too strong and a comma is too weak (check your punctuation style manual for the exact use of the dash).

Our equivalent on the typewriter was the double hyphen, but now we have a real em dash. Using two hyphens (or worse, one) where there should be an em dash makes your work look very unprofessional.

Since you were properly taught, of course, you know that the double hyphen is not supposed to have a space on either side of it—neither is the em dash, as you can see right here in this sentence. There are six other examples of the em dash in this chapter.

To type an em dash

em dash — Shift Option Hyphen
*hold the Shift and Option keys down,
then tap the hyphen key*

Special characters

Take advantage of the special characters available in all fonts on your Mac.

Consistent with the purpose of letting us create professional-level type right on our desktops, the Mac provides us with such marks as ®, TM, ¢, etc., which are the particular topic of this chapter, as well as such luxuries as accent marks that can be placed right over the letter they belong to (dealt with in the following chapter), and real quotation marks and apostrophes (see pages 15 through 20).

Key Caps

If you haven't yet looked at Key Caps, you should check it out.

> On Macs running any operating system below Mac OS X (ten), Key Caps is under the Apple menu.
>
> In Mac OS X, Key Caps is in the Utilities folder, which is inside the Applications folder.

When you open Key Caps, you see a layout of the keyboard. In the menu bar at the top of your screen you'll see a menu item called either **Key Caps** or **Font** (depending on which operating system you're using). Under that item is a list of the fonts that are loaded in your System. Choose the font you'd like to see displayed in Key Caps.

This is the utility called Key Caps. From the Key Caps menu that appeared, I chose Bailey Sans Regular, which you see here.

What you initially see are the same keys you see on your keyboard in front of you, under your fingers. If you hold down the Shift key on the keyboard, on the Key Caps layout on your screen you'll see the Shift key depressed and a *second* key layout—all the capital letters and the Shift-characters. You knew all about those two layouts already.

There are actually two more keyboard layouts available to you. Most of the characters are consistent in every font; some fonts may have more alternates available than others.

To see another keyboard layout, press the Option key down—now you see all the Option-characters available in that particular font, as shown below.

You can see, above, that the Option key is pressed down (circled). With the Option key down, the accent marks (with the white borders) are visible in this keyboard, as well as symbols like ¢, ¡, ÷, or £.

If you hold the Option and Shift keys down, you see another set of symbols (can you find the real apostrophe?). Try selecting different fonts from the Key Caps menu and viewing all the special characters belonging to the other fonts.

To use these characters in your document, follow these steps:

1. If you don't know exactly which keys will give you the desired mark, open Key Caps (if you already know which keys you need because you looked it up in Appendix B at the back of this book, then skip to Step #6).

2. From the menu item Key Caps or Fonts, choose the name of a font. You will see a keyboard layout for that font.

3. Find the character you want to use; if you don't see it on the screen immediately, press the Shift key, the Option key, or the Shift and Option keys together.

4. Notice where the character appears on the screen keyboard; find that key on the keyboard under your fingers.

5. Once you know which keys you need to create that character, **remember them** and go back to your document.

6. Set the insertion point where you want the new character to appear.

7. If the character is in a font that is different from the one you are currently using, then choose that font from your menu—otherwise, never mind.

8. Press the appropriate keys; for example, in any font, hold down the Option key and press G to get this mark: ©.

9. If the character you type is in a different font from the one you were using in your document, you will have to choose your original font again from the menu because the insertion point continues typing in whatever character is directly to its left, even if that character is a blank space. To prevent this situation:

   a. Just press the Option/Shift/character keys in whatever font you are using—some strange character will appear on your page. That's okay.

   b. When you are done with the sentence, go back to that character, select it, and change it to the font you need. The correct character will appear.

▼ If you find you need a particular character regularly— a Zapf Dingbats checkbox at the beginning of each paragraph, for example—type in the key combination along with typing the rest of the document, even though it creates a strange character on your page. Then change the first strange character to Zapf Dingbats; copy it; select the rest of the strange characters one at a time; replace them by pasting in the copied character.

Or use the search-and-replace feature in your program, if it allows you to change fonts. If so, search for the strange character and just change its font.

A list for you

Below is a list of the commonly used special characters in general typing. To create any of these, hold down the Shift and/or Option key while you press the letter for that character. See the following chapter for setting accent marks.

"   Option [opening double quote

"   Option Shift [closing double quote

'   Option]   opening single quote

'   Option Shift]   closing single quote; apostrophe

–   Option Hyphen   en dash

—   Option Shift Hyphen   em dash

…   Option ;   ellipsis (this character can't be separated at the end of a line as three periods can)

•   Option 8   bullet (easy to remember because it's the asterisk key)

fi   Option Shift 5   ligature (combination) of f and i

fl   Option Shift 6   ligature (combination) of f and l

©   Option g

™   Option 2

®   Option r

°   Option Shift 8   degree symbol (e.g., 102°F)

¢   Option $

€   Option Shift 2   Euro symbol (in newer fonts)

⁄   Option Shift 1 (one)   fraction bar (this doesn't descend below the line as the slash does)

¡   Option 1 (one)

¿   Option Shift ?

£   Option 3

ç   Option c

Ç   Option Shift c

Accent marks

Where an accent mark is appropriate, use it.

The accent marks are a little sneakier than the special characters I discussed in the previous chapter—easy, but sneaky. If you've ever tried to use the tilde key to type the word piñata with the tilde over the n, you've noticed that it doesn't work—you get pin~ata. That looks kinda silly.

This is the trick: The accent marks are all hidden on the Option keyboard. First find out (either from this chart, the chart at the end of the book, or in your Key Caps; see page 25) which letter is hiding the accent mark; typically it's the character with which the accent mark is most likely to be used.

To type an accent over a letter in your document, first hold down the Option key and hit the accent character; nothing will happen. That's good! Now, type the character you want *under* that accent mark; they will then appear together.

For example, to type **résumé**:

1. Open Key Caps. Notice on the layout that you get the accent mark ´ with the combination of the Option key and the letter **e**. Close Key Caps (**or** you could just look up the key combination in the chart).

2. Type **r**.

3. Now hold down the Option key and press the letter **e**; *nothing will happen.* That's good.

4. Now, *without* holding down the Option key, type the letter **e**; you will get **é**.

5. Repeat the sequence when you get to the last **e**.

A list of the accent marks and where to find them is on the next page, as well as in Appendix B at the end of the book.

■

These are the most common accent marks you will need. A complete
list is in Appendix B.

       ´   Option e

       `   Option ~   *(upper-left or next to the Spacebar)*

       ¨   Option u

       ~   Option n

       ^   Option i

This accent mark is only found on the letter c, so it just comes along
with the letter; there is no need to press twice:

       ç   Option c

       Ç   Option Shift c

Underlining

Never underline. Underlining is for typewriters; italic is for professional text.

Have you ever seen a word underlined in a magazine or a book? Most likely not (except for a special effect). That's because typesetters *italicize* words for emphasis or for proper convention, such as book titles, periodicals, operas, symphonies.

On a typewriter, of course, there is no way to italicize. So we were taught to underline words for emphasis, or to underline those items just mentioned—books, periodicals, etc. This underline was originally a signal to the typesetter to italicize the underlined word—and *remove* the underline). But we don't need the signal anymore; we can and should type the true italic.

Underlining in general should be avoided—the underline tends to be heavy, it's usually too close to the type, and it bumps into the "descenders" of the letters (those parts that hang below the invisible line on which type sits, as in the letters g, j, p, q, and y).

If you want to emphasize a word or two, you have other options also. Try **bold type**, larger type, or a different font.

Simply setting text apart from the rest of the copy can call extra attention to a bit of it.

This doesn't mean you should never use any sort of line with text—just don't use the underline style that appears on the menu. If your typographic design calls for a line, use a drawn line (called a "rule" in typesetter's jargon). Most word processors and all page layout, paint, and draw programs have some feature where you can draw a line

■

under a word or headline. When you *draw* a line, you can place it where you want and make it as thick or thin or long as you want. You can avoid making the line bump into the descenders. The drawn line also tends to look smoother than the underline because it is one long line, not a series of short lines hooked together.

This is an underlined phrase.

This phrase has two rules drawn beneath it.

This phrase has an *italic* word.

Capitals

Very rarely (almost never) use all capital letters.

On a typewriter, the only way to make a headline stand out was to type it in all caps or maybe underline it. Now, of course, we can make the text larger, bold, shadowed, outlined, underlined, or any gross combination of all those. We no longer need to rely on all caps to make something noticeable. And we shouldn't.

Many studies have shown that all caps are much harder to read. We recognize words not only by their letter groups, but also by their shapes, sometimes called their "coastline." Take a look at these words and their shapes:

When these words are all caps, can you tell their shapes apart?

CAT   DOG   BIGGER   PRETTY

When a word is all caps, we have to read it letter by letter, rather than by groups of letters. Try reading this block of text set in all caps; be conscious of how much slower than usual you read it and how tiring it is on your eyes.

> WEN YOU'RE A MARRIED MAN, SAMIVEL, YOU'LL UNDERSTAND A GOOD MANY THINGS AS YOU DON'T UNDERSTAND NOW; BUT VETHER IT'S WORTH WHILE GOIN' THROUGH SO MUCH TO LEARN SO LITTLE, AS THE CHARITY-BOY SAID VEN HE GOT TO THE END OF THE ALPHABET, IS A MATTER O' TASTE.

Charles Dickens, *Pickwick Papers*

■

Setting a *strange-looking* font in all caps is particularly bad practice, or setting italic or calligraphy or an italic-outlined-bold-shadowed-underlined face in reverse on a patterned background—aack! Take a look at how this font in all caps becomes almost impossible to read:

MACINTOSH MADNESS   (12 point, TypoUpright regular)

All caps also takes up a lot more space. With lowercase letters, you can make the type size bigger and bolder in the same (or less) amount of space, which will be more efficient and more effective.

Macintosh Madness   (14 point, Bailey Sans Bold)

Occasionally you may have some very good reason to use all caps in a very short block of text or in a heading. Sometimes the particular look you want on the page can only be created with all caps. When you do that, just be aware of the inherent problems; recognize that you're making a choice between a design solution and the legibility/readability of the piece. Be able to justify the choice.

A little puzzle

Here is a fun little teaser to impress upon you how much we depend on word shapes to read. On the following lines are two well-known proverbs. The letters are indicated only by black rectangles the size of each letter. Can you read the sentences? How quickly would you be able to read them if they were set this way in all caps?

1.   ▮▮▮▮'▮ ▮▮ ▮▮▮▮▮ ▮▮▮▮ ▮▮▮▮.

2.   ▮ ▮▮▮▮▮▮ ▮▮ ▮▮▮▮ ▮▮
       ▮ ▮▮▮▮▮ ▮▮▮▮▮▮.

Kerning

Adjust the space between letters according to your sensitive visual perception.

One of the most important things a professional typesetter did for a client was **kern** the type. **Kerning** is the process of removing small units of space *between letters* to create **visually consistent letterspacing.** The larger the letters, the more critical it is to adjust their spacing. Awkward letterspacing not only looks naïve and unprofessional, it can disrupt the communication of the words. Look carefully at these two examples and notice the spaces between the letters (try squinting):

WASHINGTON *unkerned*

WASHINGTON *kerned*

The secret of kerning is that *it is totally dependent on your eye, not on the machine.* In the first example, the software set each letter with the same amount of space on both sides of each letter. Some spaces *appear* to be larger because of the shapes of the letters—angled or rounded. In the second example, the software was set to adjust, or kern, the letters, and it did a fairly good job, but the letters still needed some manual adjusting, which I did. *Type needs a human eye for the fine tuning.*

Look at the square and circle below. Which one appears to be larger?

Actually, they are both exactly the same size from edge to edge. The circle *appears* to be smaller because of all the white space surrounding it. It is this fact that creates the need to manually and visually letterspace/kern type—each character presents a different visual impression on the page,

and reacts with the other letters according to their particular combinations of dark and light space. These impressions can be broken
down into a few generalized combinations:

HL   Characters with verticals next to each other need
the *most* amount of space; this can often be used as a
guideline with which to keep the spacing consistent.

HO   A vertical next to a curve needs less space.

OC   A curve next to a curve needs very little space.

OT   A curve can actually overlap into the white space under
or above the bar or stem of a character, and vice versa.

AT   The closest kerning is done where both letters have
a great deal of white space around them.

Remember, the point is to keep the spacing visually consistent—there
should visually *appear* to be the same amount of space between all
the letters. It's not critical how much, nor is it critical that it's tight or
loose—it's critical that it be **consistent.** You can usually focus better on
that white space if you look at the text with your eyes squinted.

Kerning is not possible in all applications; typically you'll find it in
page layout programs or in applications where text manipulation is
a primary feature. You won't usually find it possible to control the
kerning in a word processor, which is why you can usually glance at
text printed from a word processor and know that it was not created
in a page layout application; you might not be able to put your finger
on it, but your eye knows the letterspacing is inconsistent.

In applications that have a kerning feature, each character and space
is broken down into little sections, called *units,* anywhere from 5 to
1000 units per character. Using the kerning function, it is possible to
take out one of those units at a time between letters, allowing for very
precise positioning. Check the manual for the particular method of
kerning in your application.

Listen to your eyes.

Tabs and indents

Learn to control the tabs and indents, then use them regularly. Never use the Spacebar to align text.

You cannot use the Spacebar to line up words or numbers. That method works on a typewriter because every letter takes up the same amount of space, so five spaces is always five spaces. This is not true on a Mac because you are almost always using proportional type, as explained in Chapter 1. If you want text to align, you *must* use tabs.

Unfortunately, the tabs and indents confuse people. But once you understand how they work and can control them, you'll find it amazing what you can do. The tabs and indents do exactly what you tell them—*you* just need to learn what it is you're telling them to do!

First, two basic features to understand:

1. Every application that uses a lot of text has **rulers.** A word processors displays a ruler across the top of the screen; page layout applications hide or show the ruler as you need it for selected blocks of text.

    This is the important thing to remember: **Every paragraph has its own ruler setting.** You create a "paragraph" every time you hit the Return key. Thus a three-line address in a letter is seen by the Mac as three paragraphs; a list that is three columns wide and twenty lines deep is twenty individual paragraphs. So *when you want to apply or change the tabs or indents, you must first select every paragraph to which you want the changes to apply.*

2. Your entire document has **margins** that you set in the margin dialog box. For instance, you might have a 1.5–inch margin on the left edge of the printed page and a 1–inch margin on the right. Any **indents** you set, on the right or the left, *will be indented inward from those margins.* That is, if you set a paragraph with a 1–inch *indent* on both sides, that paragraph will now be 2.5 inches from the left edge of the printed page and 2 inches on the right. See the example on the next page. *(Page layout applications are a little different—the ruler shows the outer edges of the selected text block.)*

Indent markers and indents

Every ruler in every program that uses text has three **movable markers** in the ruler. This is what those individual markers control:

Right indent. As you type along, the text moves out to the right until it hits this marker and then it bounces back to the left.

First-line indent. When you hit a Return, the first line of the next paragraph goes to this marker.

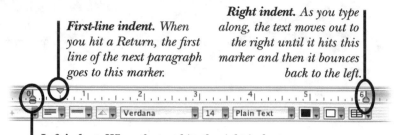

Left indent. When the text hits the right indent marker, it bounces back to this left marker.

In the example below, look carefully at the ruler and the margin markers. You can see the insertion point in the second paragraph (circled); the insertion point *selects* the paragraph, *and that paragraph's ruler settings are shown.* Notice how the first-line indent, and both the left and right indents are moved inward; notice that the text in the second paragraph aligns with these markers.

I selected the second paragraph, then dragged both the first-line indent and the left margin inward one inch.

While the second paragraph was selected, I dragged the right margin inward one inch. You can see how it affected the second paragraph.

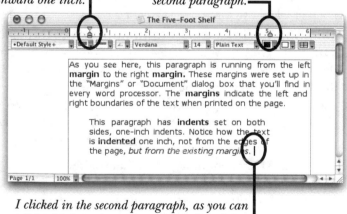

I clicked in the second paragraph, as you can tell by this insertion point, which selected that paragraph and displayed its ruler settings.

Now, if you were to click in the first paragraph in the example above, thus displaying the ruler settings for that paragraph, where would the markers be? Correct—all the way to the left and right margins.

Try it—create indents and outdents:

1. In your word processor, type two separate paragraphs (only hit the Return key at the end of a paragraph, *not at the end of every line!*).

2. Click in the first paragraph to select it, then drag the margin markers inward.

3. Click in the second paragraph and notice that the margin markers are still where they began, on the outer edges.

   This time, **move just the first-line indent inward:** Grab the *top* portion of the marker that you see on the left edge, and drag it to the right. You'll notice that just the first line of the second paragraph indents to that position.

4. Click at the end of this second paragraph, and hit a Return. Notice that the paragraph is automatically indented like the previous one. That's because of this basic feature of the Mac:

   The insertion point in every application picks up the formatting from the character to its left. So when you set the first-line indent in the second paragraph and hit a Return, you carried that formatting down into the next paragraph. This will continue until you change the ruler settings for a selected paragraph.

*Drag the top marker to the right for a first-line indent for **selected** paragraphs.*

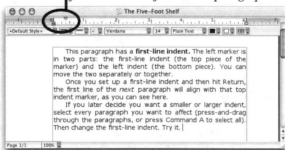

*Or do the opposite: drag the **bottom** part of the marker inward to create an outdent.*

To move the left indent separately from the first-line indent in some programs, you have to hold down the Shift key.

In the program in this example (Mariner Write), grab the pointy part of the left margin marker to drag it independently of the first-line indent.

Grab the flat bottom part to drag both the left indent and first-line indent markers together.

■

Tab markers and tabs

Every text application has at least four different tab stops and markers; some have more (check your manual). Below are examples of what the four basic markers will do. Remember this rule, though: when setting tabs, *always use a left alignment on your text* (that is, don't try to set tabs in centered or right-aligned text).

Left-aligned tab: The text lines up at the tab stop and types out to the right, so the *left* side of the text is aligned. Typically the marker has a little tail pointing to the right, in the direction the text will type.

One dog
Two dog
Big dog
Black dog

Right-aligned tab: The text lines up at the tab stop and types out to the left, so the *right* side of the text is aligned. It actually looks like it's typing backwards. Typically the marker has a little tail pointing to the left, in the direction the text will type.

One dog
Two dog
Big dog
Black dog

This is the tab to use for **columns of numbers** to keep all the ones and tens and so on in their proper columns.

493
5
1,094,320
5,672

Centered tab: The text lines up at the tab stop and *centers* itself under the tab. As you type, the text actually moves out in both directions. Typically the marker has no tail at all.

This text
is set with
a centered tab.

Decimal tab: The text lines up at the decimal place or period. As you type, the text moves out to the *left;* as soon as you hit the period or decimal, any characters following it will move out to the *right*.

45.9
12,453.056
.53
1.02

This is the tab to use for keeping dollars and cents in their proper columns, to keep the decimal point lined up when you have a varying amount of numbers following it, and to create the numbered paragraphs as shown on the following pages. Typically the marker has no tail, but a little dot next to it.

$2.45
$123.90
$45.72
$7,812.03

1. This is number one.
   . . .
9. This is number nine.
10. This is number ten.

How to set and use tabs

1. Select the paragraph(s) to which you want the tab to apply. **Or** you can set the tabs before you ever start typing.

2. Choose the kind of tab you need. The tab options might be in a tiny menu or in a little box.

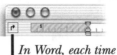

Mariner Write has a tiny menu; choose your tab, then click in the ruler.

In Word, each time you click this tiny marker it displays a different tab marker. Keep clicking to cycle to the one you need.

InDesign (above) and AppleWorks (below) display the markers.

3. Click in the ruler at the position where you want the tab stop to be. To move its position, just drag it left or right.

   If you accidentally set the wrong type of tab, drag it off the ruler to remove it. In some applications you can double-click the tiny tab marker in the ruler and it opens a dialog box where you can change the type of tab and its position.

4. To set text at that tab stop, first hit the Tab key. Then type.

5. Hit a Return. Repeat Step 4 until done.

Try it with this little exercise:

1. Set three left-aligned tabs in the ruler, with plenty of space between each tab.

2. Hit the Tab key. Type: **One**
   Hit the Tab key. Type: **Two**
   Hit the Tab key. Type: **Three**
   Hit the Return key.

   Repeat the above four steps to type the second line, as shown below. Then type the third line.

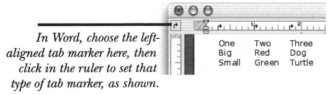

In Word, choose the left-aligned tab marker here, then click in the ruler to set that type of tab marker, as shown.

3. **Now try this:** Select all three of those lines. Drag the indent markers left and right and watch everything line up.

Two important features of tabs

There are two things you must understand or you'll go nuts.

1. There are invisible, default tabs set every half inch. *As soon as you set a tab anywhere in the ruler, all the defaults to the left of that point disappear;* default tabs are still present, available, and invisible to the right. This is the thing that will make you crazy because you don't know there are invisible tabs in the first place, so when you add one and all the invisible tabs to the left disappear, all your type goes wonky.

2. Tabs go to the **first available tab** they can find (which might not be the first tab in the ruler). And **tabs accumulate,** as shown below.

Every text application has a menu item or a preference where you can turn on the "invisible" or "hidden" characters so you can see them. Here the Tab keys are shown as tiny arrows.

The Five-Foot Shelf

Verdana   14   Plain Text

a.→	Jennifer→	Laura→	Timothy→	Reese
b.→	Sue→→	Joe→ →	Ruby→	Larry
c.→	Ann→→	Debra→	Dana→	Joannie

This is a common problem: You type, trying to align things in columns, but you don't realize there are invisible tabs and so sometimes you hit one tab, and sometimes you hit two. **Tabs accumulate:** Above, each tiny arrow indicates hitting the Tab key. You can see that Jennifer has been told to go to the first tab, Laura to the second, Tim to the third, and Reese to the fourth (count the arrows to their left). On the second line, you can see *two* tab characters after Sue and also after Joe, which means Ruby will go to the fifth tab *she can find,* and Larry to the sixth. They are going to the **invisible tab markers** set every half inch. Now as soon as you start putting your own tabs in the ruler and the invisible ones to the left disappear, everything goes nuts, as shown below!

*Here you can see that Joe is doing just as he was told—he's going to the third tab! And Ruby is going to the fifth tab, which is at the 4" mark since **there is still an invisible tab marker at that point.** That is the fifth tab **she can find.** See, they are doing exactly what I told them!*

These are the four tabs I inserted.

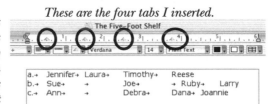

The Five-Foot Shelf

Verdana   14   Plain Text

a.→	Jennifer→	Laura→	Timothy→	Reese
b.→	Sue→	→	Joe→	→ Ruby→ Larry
c.→	Ann→	→	Debra→	Dana→ Joannie

Can you see why Debra, Dana, and Joannie are in the wrong columns? Delete the extra tab between Ann and Debra and the other three will align properly.

So follow this simple rule: **only hit one tab between columns of type.** Even if things don't line up at first, don't ever hit more Tab keys—*select the lines* and adjust the tab markers in the ruler instead.

Practice by setting the example shown below. **Hint:** Type each line, hitting ONE tab between each item. *It doesn't matter right now if they don't line up!* Hit a Return at the end of each line. Make sure your text is flush left (that is, not centered, etc.). It should look something like this:

You do not need a tab before the items in the first column. Notice each item is aligning with the next half-inch tab marker it can find.

Name	Task	Due Date	
Ryan	Write the poetry book		December 2
Jimmy	Paint the fresco	April 19	
Scarlett	Produce the documentary		May 1

Press Command A to **select all** of your text. In your ruler, set a left-aligned tab for the "Task" column and one for the "Due Date" column. Drag the tab markers left or right until your text lines up cleanly. Obviously, the "Due Date" tab needs to be far enough to the right of "Task" to allow space for the items. If, later in your list, you add a longer task, *select all of the lines,* then move the tab markers again.

In this example, I also moved the first-line indent inward so the items in the first column are a little indented. By using the indent, I don't have to type a tab before each item in the first column.

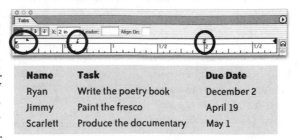

Name	**Task**	**Due Date**
Ryan	Write the poetry book	December 2
Jimmy	Paint the fresco	April 19
Scarlett	Produce the documentary	May 1

Here are the ruler settings for one of the most common type settings, the **indented, bulleted paragraph.** Type the bullet (Option 8), *hit the Tab key,* then type your paragraph. *Do not hit Return until you are ready for the next bullet!* After a couple of bulleted paragraphs, select all of the paragraphs, and simply drag the *left indent* marker inward. Amazing.

In almost all applications, the Tab key will go to the left indent marker, as shown here. If it doesn't in your application (like PageMaker), set a left-aligned tab directly on top of the indent marker.

• What you should NEVER do is hit a Return at the end of the line, and then space over to line up the text.

• Nor should you set the paragraph, then go back and hit the Tab key to make the second and third lines indented. Stop that!

Here are the tab settings for another of the most common text settings, but one that seems to cause the most confusion: **numbered blocks of text,** especially when the numbers go above ten.

Once you know how to control the tabs and indents, you will never create a faux pas like this again!

. . . .
9.| This is WRONG. As you well know, decimal points should line up. Numbers need to align on the right side—the numeral "9" should *not* be aligned over the "1" in the numeral 10.

10.| **The trick is this:** you must set a decimal tab so the numbers align, which means you need to hit a tab *before* you type the number.

Do it this way (don't worry how it lines up at the moment!):

1. Hit the Tab key.
    Type the number 1 and a period.
    Hit the Tab key again.
    Type your paragraph. Do not hit Return until you are finished with your paragraph.

2. Hit the Tab key.
    Type the number 2 and a period.
    Hit the Tab key again.
    Type your paragraph; when done, hit the Return key.

3. Continue (or skip) to number 10. Repeat the above steps.
    (If you like, add the number 104 to the mix, setting it as above).
    Your text probably looks something like this:

As long as you hit only one tab between items, you can rest assured that you will always be able to adjust the tab markers to make things align properly.

1.   First paragraph. Don't worry about how things are lining up—trust me, it will all line up perfectly in a minute.

2.   Yes, it is a little nerve-wracking that it appears so wrong. Let go. Breathe deeply.

. . . .

104.   This paragraph is the big test. As you can see, I am pretending I have a very long list that goes up to 104.

4. Select all of your text.

5. In the ruler, put a decimal tab at about ¼-inch.

6. Move the *left indent marker* (the bottom part) to the *right* of the decimal tab, to about ½-inch. Oh my gosh, it works.

*Remember, if you're using a program that does not send the tab to the indent marker, set a left-aligned tab **directly** on top of the indent marker.*

1. First paragraph. Don't worry about how things are lining up—it will all align perfectly in a minute.

. . . .

104. What did I tell you? Isn't this lovely?

Widows and orphans

Obviously, this term isn't referring to bereaved widows and orphans such as some of us are ourselves—no, these are actually traditional, technical, typographic terms.

When a paragraph ends and leaves fewer than seven characters (not words, characters) on the last line, that last line is called a **widow.** Worse than leaving *one* word at the end of a line is leaving *part* of a word, the other part being hyphenated on the line above.

> A gentle joyousness—a mighty
> mildness of repose in swiftness,
> invested the gliding whale. Not the
> white bull Jupiter swimming away
> with ravished Europa clinging to
> his graceful horns; his lovely, leering
> eyes sideways intent upon the maid;
> with smooth bewitching fleetness,
> rippling straight for the nuptial bower
> in Crete; not Jove, not that great
> majesty Supreme! did surpass the
> glorified White Whale as he so divinely

widow → swam.

> On each soft side—
> coincident with the
> parted swell, that but
> once leaving him, then
> flowed so wide away—
> on each bright side,
> the whale shed off en-

an even worse widow → ticings.

■

When the last line of a paragraph, be it ever so long, won't fit at the bottom of a column and must end itself at the top of the next column, that is an **orphan.**

| orphan
↓

. . . Moby Dick moved on, still withholding from sight the full terrors of his submerged trunk, entirely hiding the wrenched hideousness of his jaw. But soon the fore part of him slowly rose from the water; for an instant his whole marbleized body formed a high arch, like Virginia's Natural Bridge, and warningly waving his bannered flukes in the air, the grand god revealed himself, sounded, and went out of sight. Hoveringly halting, and dipping on the wing, the white sea-fowls longingly lingered over the agitated pool

that he left.

With oars apeak, and paddles down, the sheets of their sails adrift, the three boats now stilly floated, awaiting Moby Dick's appearance.

In long Indian file, as when herons take wing, the white birds were now all flying towards Ahab's boat; and when within a few yards began fluttering over the water there, wheeling round and round, with joyous, expectant cries.

Herman Melville, *Moby Dick*

Avoid both of these situations. If you have editing privileges, rewrite the copy, or at least add or delete a word or two. Sometimes you can remove spacing from the letters, words, or lines, depending on which program you're working in. Sometimes widening a margin just a hair will do it. But it must be done. Widows and orphans on a page are tacky.

See what I mean?

Hyphenations and line breaks

Avoid stupid hyphenations.
Avoid more than two hyphenations in a row.
Avoid too many hyphenations in any paragraph.
Never hyphenate a heading.
Break lines sensibly.

It's amazing how often silly line breaks show up. A line break is simply that—where a heading or sentence breaks off at the end of a line.

This is more often critical in headings or in short blocks of text than in long manuscripts, although even in lengthy text you can find those classic cases, like hyphenating the word *therapist* so it becomes *the- rapist.* We've all seen strange hyphenations like turn-ed, or-phans, occurren-ce. Some, obviously, are downright wrong. Not only are they wrong, they're a gross sign of unprofessionalism. Watch them. Don't rely on your software package to do it the best way. Use a dictionary to verify any word that looks a bit odd. Read the lines carefully; even if a word is broken properly, pick up on any instances where there may be a split second of confusion, ambiguity, racism, sexism, stupidity, etc., resulting from breaking the line at that particular point. If there is, fix it. Notice how awkward these sentences are (these actually came back from a professional typesetter):

> **SRJC is an open-access cam-**
> **pus.**

> **Any prospective or interested stud-**
> **ent can contact the Instructional Office.**

When there's room, don't hyphenate

It's amazing how often I see captions where there is plenty of room to set the entire word without hyphenating, but someone was visually unconscious. Please watch for these kinds of problems:

> *With intricate, hand-carved etchings and detailed knotwork, this ancient lyre celebrates a living legacy.*

> *Frogs represent wealth, abundance, and prosperity in Celtic tradition.*

Avoid more than two hyphenations in a row

Almost as bad as dumb hyphenations are too many hyphenations in a row. Sometimes you can't avoid hyphenating, but it's never necessary to hyphenate three times in a row, or six of the eight lines in a paragraph. In those cases, you really must adjust something. I prefer no more than one hyphenation per *paragraph,* when possible.

Often, too many hyphenations are the result of using a justified alignment (text aligned on both sides of the column, as this is) on a line that is too short for the point size. If it's not possible to left-align the text, try rewording, adjusting letter or word spacing if that's possible, kerning (see Chapter 9), widening the margin, or pressing Shift Return before the offending word on a justified line to bump it down to the next line.

Never hyphenate words in a headline

All headlines can be broken at logical points. Even though you should not have *any* hyphenations in a headline, insensitive line breaks can still make your text awkward or ambiguous.

Generally, group lines of a heading into appropriate grammatical sections. Which of the following would be more appropriate?

Jimmy's Lemonade **Stand**	**Jimmy's** **Lemonade Stand**
Parade in the Bay **Area was a Success**	**Parade in the Bay Area** **was a Success**
The Theater presents Don **Quixote de la Mancha**	**The Theater presents** **Don Quixote de la Mancha**

■

Watch line breaks in body text as well

Most of the text you create is flush left with a "ragged" right margin. Try to keep the right margin as even as possible, both for the visual effect as well as for smoother reading—it can be bothersome to have lines ending at radically different points. This means you may need to bump words from one line down to the next line, or occasionally rewrite copy to adjust the lines.

> Few things are pure, and they are seldom simple; and
> of all the impure and unsimple things in this world
> which befog and bedevil the minds of men, their
> ideas about women deserve to take first place.
>
> —Oscar *Wilde*

> Few things are pure, and they are seldom simple;
> and of all the impure and unsimple things in this
> world which befog and bedevil the minds of men,
> their ideas about women deserve to take first place.
>
> —*Oscar Wilde*

Do you notice how the second example has a smoother right edge? Simply bumping the word 'and' from the first line to the second (by pressing Shift Return in front of the word) rearranged all the following lines to give a smoother right margin. Then I also aligned "Oscar Wilde" with the last line in the text, rather than with the outer margin because your eye *sees* the connection to the last line; it does not see the connection to the invisible margin.

> O, that my tongue were
> in the thunder's mouth!
> Then with a passion would I
> shake the world.
>
> *Constance* in *King John*

The word "I" hanging off the end of a line always looks so lost and lonely. Bump it down.

> O, that my tongue were
> in the thunder's mouth!
> Then with a passion would
> I shake the world.
>
> *Constance* in *King John*

Leading, or linespace

■

Keep the linespacing consistent.

Linespacing within a paragraph should be consistent. We often set an initial cap or a word in a larger point size than the rest of the text. In many software programs this affects the linespacing, or leading (the space between the lines of type); if even one letter or word is larger, the linespacing adjusts to fit the larger character(s), creating uneven spacing.

The history of the term leading (pronounced *ledding*) may give you a better grasp of what leading itself accomplishes and how you can best adjust it.

Until the early 1970s, all printed type was set in hot metal. Each letter—each and every little letter—was cast onto a tiny piece of lead *backwards* so when printed the letter would be facing the right direction. All these letters were lined up in a row, with other tiny pieces of blank metal stuck between the words to separate them. Even the newer (1884) Linotype machines (which composed whole lines of metal type at a time instead of one letter at a time) used the same principle. Between each line of type another piece of blank *lead* was inserted to separate the lines—this was called the *leading*.

Now, the type was measured in points, just like the type on the Mac (72 points per inch). The leading was also measured in points. If the type was **10** points high and the little piece of lead inserted between the lines was **2** points high, then the **2** points was *added onto* the point size of the type and the leading was called **12** point. Got that?

10 point type on
2 points of linespace
makes 12 pt. leading

*This was actually a piece of lead 2 points thick. **Adding** the leading to the point size of the type is what gives you the leading options you see in your menu, such as 12, 14, 18, etc.; it's not actually 18 points of blank space.*

Automatic leading, or linespacing

Typically, a standard unit of measure for the leading between the lines is 20 percent of the point size: in the example on the previous page, the type is 10 point, the leading would be 12 point. (Many Macintosh programs call this value 120 percent, which is the same as adding on the 20 percent.)

What all this boils down to is that when you type on the Mac, you automatically get a 20 percent leading (that's **auto leading**). When you make a word or character larger, in many programs it automatically shows up with more leading. This creates an awkward look to a paragraph, as then one line has more space after it than the others. For instance, if you use 12-point type, the auto leading is around 14 (about 120 percent of the point size). But when you insert a 24-point initial letter into your paragraph, the leading for that one line automatically bumps up to about 29.

In this example, the first letter of the paragraph is larger and disrupts the even linespacing of the rest of the paragraph.

This paragraph also has a large initial cap, but I adjusted the leading value. Now all of the lines have an equal amount of space between them.

Correct the linespacing

It's usually possible to correct the line spacing, depending on the program you're creating it in.

- If your application allows you to adjust the leading, then select the entire paragraph and reset the leading to what it originally was for the *smaller* type.

- Sometimes you can adjust the leading, but it won't let you go smaller than the auto-leading for the larger size, the one that's disruptive; in that case you'll need to adjust the line spacing for the entire paragraph to match the *larger* size.

- If you're having difficulty fixing the leading in a page layout program, you may find it easier to set the initial cap in its own text block and move it in next to the rest of the text as a separate unit.

- If you're using an application that doesn't let you adjust the line spacing at all, you can sneak in this trick: select one of the blank spaces between the words on a line; change the point size of the blank space to the same size as the large initial cap or word that's causing all this trouble. You'll have to do this separately for each line in the paragraph in order to make them all match.

Adjust leading with all caps

You'll find extra, awkward leading between lines of all capital letters (on those rare occasions when you use all caps!). That's because caps have no "descenders"—those parts of the lowercase letters g, j, p, q, and y that drop below the rest of the letters.

To tighten up the leading, figure out what the auto leading is (120 percent of the point size). Then set the leading to less than that. For instance, the auto leading for 36-point type would be about 43; reset it for less than 43. Usually on all caps you can actually reduce it to less than the number of the point size of the type; e.g., 36-point type and 34-point leading—try it!

Notice that the example below uses "negative" leading (leading less than the point value of the type).

TOO MUCH LINESPACE

(18-point type; auto leading, which would be 21.6)

LINESPACING ADJUSTED

(18-point type; 16-point leading)

The same is true of a headline in lowercase that has few descenders. Without descenders to fill in the space between the two lines, the gap appears much larger than necessary.

This has too much Spacing

(18-point type; auto leading)

This has Better Linespacing

(18-point type; 16-point leading)

Paragraph spacing

Adjust the space between paragraphs.
Don't indent first paragraphs.

Never hit two Returns between paragraphs

To have more space between paragraphs on a typewriter, our only option was to hit the carriage return twice. You've probably noticed in Macintosh typesetting that this turns out to be an excessive amount, giving a clunky look to your paragraphs, as shown below. In fact, the double Return separates them so much they don't even seem to belong together, but each element appears as an independent unit.

Says Emelia

And thereof came it that the man was mad—the venomous clamours of a jealous woman poisons more deadly than a mad dog's tooth. It seems his sleeps were hindered by thy railing, and thereof comes it that his head is light.

Thou say'st his meat was sauced with thy upbraidings. Unquiet meals make ill digestions. Thereof the raging fire of fever bred, and what's a fever but a fit of madness?

Thou say'st his sports were hindered by thy brawls. Sweet recreation barred, what doth ensue but moody and dull melancholy, kinsman to grim and comfortless despair, and at her heels a huge infectious troop of pale distemperatures and foes to life?

In food, in sport, and life-preserving rest to be disturbed would madden man or beast. The consequence is, then, thy jealous fits hath scared thy husband from the use of wits.

Emelia the Abbess in *The Comedy of Errors*

Adjust the paragraph spacing

Most software applications that use type, such as word processing or page layout programs, have a feature that allows you to separate paragraphs by as many or as few points as you would like. Generally it is found in a "Paragraph" command.

This is a typical "Paragraph" dialog box (this one is from Mariner Write, a great word processor).

Spacing "After" will add that many points between the paragraphs.

Wherever you find this feature in the particular application you are using, you can add a few points in a box usually called **after.** These few points *after* mean that whenever you press Return, those few points will be *added onto* the leading used in the previous paragraph before going on to the next paragraph. If you are using 10-point type with 12-point leading, you can add 5 points after, creating about half a linespace between paragraphs. The text you are reading right here is set at 10/13 with 6 extra points between the paragraphs.

Use paragraph space *before* for headlines and subheads to put a little more space *above* the heads and subheads, which visually makes the head or subhead connect to the text *below* it, as shown below, right.

Says Emelia

And thereof came it that the man was mad—the venomous clamours of a jealous woman poisons more deadly than a mad dog's tooth.

Thou say'st his meat was sauced with thy upbraid-ings. Unquiet meals make ill digestions. Thereof the raging fire of fever bred, and what's a fever but a fit of madness?

In food, in sport, and life-preserving rest to be disturbed would mad man or beast. The consequence is, then, thy jealous fits hath scared thy husband from the use of wits.

Says Rosaline

A jest's propserity lies in the ear of him that hears it, never in the tongue of him that makes it. Then, if sickly ears, deafed with the clamours of their own dear groans, will hear your idle scorns, continue then, and I will have you and that fault withal.
But if they will not, throw away that spirit, and I shall find you empty of that fault, right joyful of your reformation.

This text has double Returns after each paragraph and after the subhead. Squint, then count how many different elements there are.

Says Emelia

And thereof came it that the man was mad—the venomous clamours of a jealous woman poisons more deadly than a mad dog's tooth.

Thou say'st his meat was sauced with thy upbraid-ings. Unquiet meals make ill digestions. Thereof the raging fire of fever bred, and what's a fever but a fit of madness?

In food, in sport, and life-preserving rest to be disturbed would mad man or beast. The consequence is, then, thy jealous fits hath scared thy husband from the use of wits.

Says Rosaline

A jest's propserity lies in the ear of him that hears it, never in the tongue of him that makes it. Then, if sickly ears, deafed with the clamours of their own dear groans, will hear your idle scorns, continue then, and I will have you and that fault withal.

But if they will not, throw away that spirit, and I shall find you empty of that fault, right joyful of your reformation.

*This text has space **after** each paragraph, and space **before** each head and subhead. Notice how unified the different elements become.*

Paragraph indents are not five spaces

On a typewriter we were taught that a paragraph indent should be five spaces or a half-inch, so we would always set a tab for that paragaraph indent accordingly. Now we can set a first-line indent, right? But the size of that five-space or half-inch indent is no longer appropriate with the professional, proportional type we are now using—it is large and clunky. This is in large part due to the fact that our type is no longer spanning the width of an 8.5 x 11–inch page, as on the typewriters.

Traditional typesetting standards set a paragraph indent of **one em** (a space equal to the point size of the type being used; that is, in 12-point type an em space is 12 points wide). Visually, this is roughly equivalent to two spaces, or the width of a capital letter M. If your program does not allow you to specify points for indents, just use a sensitive approximation.

Really, this is true—check the paragraph indents in any professionally typeset book on your shelf.

Don't indent the first paragraph

First paragraphs are not indented. The purpose of an indent is to tell the reader a new paragraph has begun. Well, if it's the first paragraph, duh. This is a difficult guideline to get used to, I admit, but once you get used to it you'll recognize it as "right" and can be righteously affronted when you see it done wrong.

Says Emelia

And thereof came it that the man was mad—the venomous clamours of a jealous woman poisons more deadly than a mad dog's tooth. It seems his sleeps were hindered by thy railing, and thereof comes it that his head is light.

Thou say'st his sports were hindered by thy brawls. Sweet recreation barred, what doth ensue but moody and dull melancholy, kinsman to grim and comfortless despair, and at her heels a huge infectious troop of pale distemperatures and foes to life?

In food, in sport, and life-preserving rest to be disturbed would mad man or beast. The consequence is, then, thy jealous fits hath scared thy husband from the use of wits.

Says Rosaline

A jest's propserity lies in the ear of him that hears it, never in the tongue of him that makes it. Then, if sickly ears, deafed with the clamours of their own dear groans, will hear your idle scorns, continue then, and I will have you and that fault withal.

But if they will not, throw away that spirit, and I shall find you empty of that fault, right joyful of your reformation.

A "first paragraph" includes the text beneath a headline or a subhead, since they are both the first paragraphs of the new sections.

These indents of about one em space are sufficient to alert the reader that a new paragraph begins.

∎

Use extra paragraph space or an indent, but not both

To indicate a new paragraph to a reader, you need to use **either** extra space between the paragraphs **or** an indent. You don't need both! The extra space tells the reader, "This is a new paragraph." If you also add an indent, that tells the reader, "Just in case you didn't get it, this is a new paragraph!" Your readers aren't that dumb—one visual clue is all they need.

Says Emelia

And thereof came it that the man was mad—the venomous clamours of a jealous woman poisons more deadly than a mad dog's tooth. It seems his sleeps were hindered by thy railing, and thereof comes it that his head is light.

Thou say'st his meat was sauced with thy upbraidings. Unquiet meals make ill digestions. Thereof the raging fire of fever bred, and what's a fever but a fit of madness?

Thou say'st his sports were hindered by thy brawls. Sweet recreation barred, what doth ensue but moody and dull melancholy, kinsman to grim and comfortless despair, and at her heels a huge infectious troop of pale distemperatures and foes to life?

In food, in sport, and life-preserving rest to be disturbed would mad man or beast. The consequence is, then, thy jealous fits hath scared thy husband from the use of wits.

Says Emelia

And thereof came it that the man was mad—the venomous clamours of a jealous woman poisons more deadly than a mad dog's tooth. It seems his sleeps were hindered by thy railing, and thereof comes it that his head is light.

Thou say'st his meat was sauced with thy upbraidings. Unquiet meals make ill digestions. Thereof the raging fire of fever bred, and what's a fever but a fit of madness?

Thou say'st his sports were hindered by thy brawls. Sweet recreation barred, what doth ensue but moody and dull melancholy, kinsman to grim and comfortless despair, and at her heels a huge infectious troop of pale distemperatures and foes to life?

In food, in sport, and life-preserving rest to be disturbed would maddden or man or beast. The consequence is, then, thy jealous fits hath scared thy husband from the use of wits.

This short story uses indents to indicate new paragraphs.

This short story uses space between the paragraphs.

Says Emelia

And thereof came it that the man was mad—the venomous clamours of a jealous woman poisons more deadly than a mad dog's tooth. It seems his sleeps were hindered by thy railing, and thereof comes it that his head is light.

Thou say'st his meat was sauced with thy upbraidings. Unquiet meals make ill digestions. Thereof the raging fire of fever bred, and what's a fever but a fit of madness?

Thou say'st his sports were hindered by thy brawls. Sweet recreation barred, what doth ensue but moody and dull melancholy, kinsman to grim and comfortless despair, and at her heels a huge infectious troop of pale distemperatures and foes to life?

In food, in sport, and life-preserving rest to be disturbed would mad man or beast. The consequence is, then, thy jealous fits hath scared thy husband from the use of wits.

As you can see here, it is redundant to use indents and space between the paragraphs—choose one.

Justified text

Justify text only if the line is long enough to prevent awkward and inconsistent word spacing.

The power of a word processor is so much fun that it's easy to go overboard. The tendency is to do all those things we couldn't do on a typewriter (if you're old enough to have actually used a typewriter), and one of the most common things is to justify all the text (that is, to align it on both margins, like this paragraph). On a few kinds of typewriters it was possible to do this with a great deal of trouble, and heaven forbid if you made a typo and had to go back later and correct it. But with our magic computers, a push of a button and the entire body of text aligns itself. It's irresistible.

Resist it. The only time you can safely get away with justifying text is if your type is small enough and your line is long enough, as in books where the text goes all the way across the page. If your line is shorter, as in newsletter, or if you don't have many words on the line, then as the type aligns to the margins the words space themselves to accommodate it. It usually looks awkward. You've seen newspaper columns where all text is justified, often with a word stretching all the way across the column, or a little word on either side of the column with a big gap in the middle. Gross. But that's what can happen with justified type. When you do it, the effect might not be as radical as the newspaper column, but if your lines are relatively short, you will inevitably end up with uncomfortable gaps in some lines, while other lines will be all squished together:

A traveller! By my faith, you have great reason to be sad: I fear you have sold your own lands to see other men's; then, to have seen much and to have nothing, is to have rich eyes and poor hands."

Rosalind
W. Shakespeare

When the spaces between the words become greater than the spaces between the lines, it creates what are called "rivers" running through the type.

When your work comes out of the printer, turn it upside down and squint at it. The rivers will be very easy to spot. Get rid of them. Try squinting at the example on the bottom of the previous page.

Here is a general guideline for determining if your line length is long enough to satisfactorily justify the text: the line length in picas should be about twice the point size of the type; that is, if the type you are using is 12 point, the line length should be at least 24 picas (24 picas is 4 inches—simply divide the number of picas by 6, as there are 6 picas per inch). Thus 9-point type should be on an 18-pica line (3 inches) before you try to justify it, and 18-point type should be on a 36-pica line (6 inches). The rulers in most programs can be changed to picas, if you like.

In some applications (like Mariner Write, shown here) you can Control-click on the ruler to change the measurement units. In others you need to check the preferences.

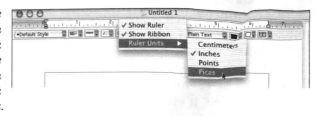

Justified text was the style for many years—we grew up on it. But there has been a great deal of research on readability (how easy something is to read) and it shows that those disruptive, inconsistent gaps between the words inhibit the flow of reading. Besides, they look dumb. Keep your eyes open as you look at professionally printed work (magazines, newsletters, annual reports, journals) and you'll find there's a very strong trend to align type on the left and leave the right ragged.

Isn't that an odd thing to read as you see this whole book justified? But it's just like the choice to use all caps: when you choose to justify type, you must realize you are choosing that *look* and sacrificing the most effective word spacing. Depending on the project, one may be more important than the other. For this book, I wanted the clean *look* of the justified line and I felt the line length was long enough to give me a minimum amount of awkward word spacing (although I must admit I still find the uneven word spacing irritating, even on this length of line; I can't have everything, they tell me).

Hanging the punctuation

Hang punctuation off the aligned edge
to eliminate any visual interruption of the text.

Hanging the punctuation is particularly important in larger sizes of text, such as headlines, or in quoted material, no matter what its size. The easiest way to explain the concept is by example. Below, notice how the quotation mark visually interrupts the left alignment. The first line appears to be indented rather than flush left.

> **"When I get a little money,**
> **I buy books.**
> **If there is any left over,**
> **I buy food and clothes."**
>
> *Desiderius Erasmus*

The block of text below has been adjusted to keep the left alignment visually intact—the quotation mark has been *hung* off the left edge.

> **"When I get a little money,**
> **I buy books.**
> **If there is any left over,**
> **I buy food and clothes."**
>
> *Desiderius Erasmus*

Notice below how even something as small as a period can create a visual misalignment.

> **Thou art thy mother's glass**
> **and she in thee**
> **Calls back the lovely April**
> **of her prime.**
>
> *William Shakespeare*

■

Hanging the period off of the right edge preserves the strength of the alignment.

Thou art thy mother's glass
and she in thee
Calls back the lovely April
of her prime.
William Shakespeare

Squint at any text that has a strong flush alignment and notice where the alignment is broken with punctuation. Look at hyphens, periods, commas, single or double quotation marks, bullets—anything that creates a slight break in the visual continuity. Then hang it.

Different software applications let you do this in different ways (some, such as Adobe InDesign and Macromedia FreeHand, can do it for you automatically). In many applications it's just not possible, as in most word processing programs. You will need to check with the manual for your particular program.

In some cases, like a quote that is set by itself, you can use an *outdent* to easily hang the punctuation. That is, set the left margin marker to the *left* of the left indent marker (see Chapter 10 on *Tabs and indents*). That's what I did on the first example on the previous page.

Inserting *non-breaking spaces* is another way to hang punctuation in a short block of text. In the second example, I inserted a *thin space* at the end of each of the first three lines, and added two thins after the by-line, since the by-line is a smaller point size (ens, ems, and thins are proportional to the size of type). A thin space takes up about one-fourth the amount of room as an em space. Generally, only page layout applications like PageMaker or InDesign can set a thin space; check the manual.

Some applications (page layout and illustration programs) allow you to pick up the letters and marks, one by one, and place them wherever you like. Occasionally it may be easiest to set the offending line in a block of its own and manually hang the entire line.

Whichever method you use, hanging the punctuation is obviously one of the last touches of detailing to do in a document. But it really must be done.

Serif and sans serif fonts

*Serif type is more **readable** and is best for text; sans serif type is more **legible** and is best used for headlines and signage.*

Type can generally be classified into two major groups: serif and sans serif. Those little ditties at the ends of the strokes of the letter are serifs. If a font doesn't have those, it's called "sans serif" ("sans" means "without" in French).

Readability

Many studies show that **serif type** is more **readable** in extended text than sans serif. It's not clear exactly why; suggestions are that the serifs tend to lead the eye along the horizontal line, or that the thick/thin variations in the strokes of most serif type eases reading, or perhaps simply the fact that we all grew up learning to read from books that used serif type. Whatever the reason, it has been well-established that serif type is easier to read in extended text. Have you ever seen a novel printed in sans serif type? (I have, and it was a dreadful experience.)

Legibility

Sans serif type, on the other hand, has been shown to be more **legible.** Legibility refers more to *character recognition* than to reading large blocks of text: sans serif is easier to recognize at a glance for short little bursts of type, as in headlines on a page, in a signage system in corporate headquarters, or the freeway signs that need to be read quickly. A full page set in sans serif may initially *appear* to be easier to read, but in the long run it proves to be tedious.

■

General use

Make a point to notice how serif and sans serif fonts are used in publications. Very typically you'll find that headlines are set in sans serif and the main body of text is set in serif. That's because it's a time-tested and infinitely variable solution.

Sans serif in text

If you do insist on setting your body text in a sans serif, keep these things in mind to improve its readability:

- Use a shorter line length (see page 60 regarding line length).
- Set not more than seven or eight words on the line (serif type can handle ten to twelve words).
- Avoid manipulating the type style to make it even less readable; i.e., use as few bold, italic, outlined, or shadowed words as possible.

Examples

Read this paragraph and the following one while trying to be particularly sensitive to which one feels a touch easier to read. Remember, *readability* becomes more important in lengthy text, such as a book or thesis paper, rather than in a paragraph or two of advertisement copy, but you can probably get a sense for it even in these short blocks. (This typeface is ITC New Baskerville.)

When the term legibility is discussed, it's referring to display type, such as headlines or signs. Read the following headlines, noticing which one is more distinguishable at a quick glance. Of course, you can *read* both of them, but once you become aware of the subtle differences in readability and legibility, you begin to have a clue as to how important the selection of a particular typeface can be to effective communication. (This typeface is Myriad Roman.)

STOP HERE

STOP HERE

Combining typefaces

Unless you have a background in design and typography, never combine more than two typefaces on the same page.

Never combine two serif fonts on the same page, and never combine two sans serif fonts on the same page.

When all those typefaces are staring at you from the Font menu and all it takes is a click of the mouse to change from one to the other, it's hard to hold yourself under control and not make the page look like a ransom note.

Try.

You can't go too wrong if you keep it down to two typefaces in a document. A particularly good combination is to use a sans serif for headings and a serif for the body copy (see the previous chapter). Now, within each typeface, it's fine to make some of it bold or italic or playful occasionally (try to keep the style you choose consistent with the purpose and meaning of the text).

Combining two san serifs

Just about never should you combine two sans serif typefaces on the same page, like Helvetica (Arial) and Avant Garde. Without going into a lot of design theory, the basic principle is that there is not enough contrast between the faces—they are too similar to each other and set up a subtle conflict. The combination will make your page look tacky and unprofessional.

Helvetica and Avant Garde do not have enough contrast between them to look good together on one page. They have very subtle differences in the shapes of the letters: Avant Garde is very geometric, while Helvetica has more classic shapes.

Helvetica

But the *similarities* between these two faces (both being sans serif) create a situation where there is neither **concord,** where all elements are working together, nor **contrast,** where elements intentionally contrast and strengthen each other. The result is **conflict.**

Avant Garde

Notice how the two sans serifs on the previous page compete with each other—they have some similarities and some differences, but not enough of either to work effectively together.

Combining two serifs

Combining two serif typefaces can be done more easily, but again, it takes some visual literacy to understand how to do it effectively.

This is the typeface **Baskerville.** It's technically considered to be a "transitional" typeface between the oldstyle and the modern.

Now this typeface is **Garamond,** a classic oldstyle. These two faces are a bad combination because they are *too similar.* The problems with type combinations always lie in the similarities!

So choose combinations of typefaces that are very different.

This face, Poster Bodoni, is different enough to be a good combination!

Or a script is often a good combination with any of the other three faces I just named. Viva la difference! (This is Lucida Handwriting.)

The safe and easy route

If you have no background in design or typography, then it is very safe to stick to two typefaces, one serif and one **sans serif.** Even though you may be saying to yourself right now, "I'm not designing anything anyway," you are. Every time you turn on your Macintosh and create a document to be printed, you're designing the page that's going to come out. If it's a newsletter, a poster, an ad, a thesis paper, an essay, or even a letter to Grandma, you are designing that page. And how you design it affects the impression it gives people. There's no reason on earth not to make that page look good.

The fun and exhilarating route

When combining typefaces, don't be a wimp. The key is in the **contrast.** Contrast with strength. Contrast with power. If one face is light and airy, choose a dense black one to go with it. If one face is small, make the other one large. If you set one all caps, set the other lowercase. If one is roman (straight up and down), combine it with a script.

Avoid weak contrasts, such as a semi-bold type with a bold type; avoid combining a script with an italic because they're both sort of curvy; don't combine large type with almost-as-large type. Put some chutzpah into it!

Othou pale Orb that silent shines
While care-untroubled mortals sleep.
Robert Burns

This is the beginnings of a contrast of type (in the initial letter Bailey Sans O), but still much too wimpy.

Othou pale Orb that silent shines
While care-untroubled mortals sleep.
Robert Burns

This is getting braver and more interesting, but try another typeface.

thou pale Orb that silent shines
While care-untroubled mortals sleep.
Robert Burns

This is a nice combination of differences, which creates a nice contrast.

*thou pale Orb that silent shines
While care-untroubled mortals sleep.*
Robert Burns

Contrast doesn't always have to include more than one typeface. Here only one typeface is used in the quote (Arcana) , but one letter is much, much larger and shaded back to a pale gray, thus contrasting in size and in color.

Below are just a few examples of how combining typefaces can enhance the communication of text, as well as make it more visually interesting. When text is more visually interesting, it's more likely to be read because it draws the viewer's eye to the page.

Hormone Derange
O gummier hum
Warder buffer-lore rum
Enter dare enter envelopes ply,
Ware soiled'em assured
    adage cur-itching ward
An disguise earn it clotty oil die.

Harm, hormone derange,
Warder dare enter envelopes ply,
Ware soiled'em assured
    adage cur-itching ward
An disguise earn it clotty oil die.

Hormone Derange
O gummier hum
Warder buffer-lore rum
Enter dare enter envelopes ply,
Ware soiled'em assured
    adage cur-itching ward
An disguise earn it clotty oil die.

Harm, hormone derange,
Warder dare enter envelopes ply,
Ware soiled'em assured
    adage cur-itching ward
An disguise earn it clotty oil die.

These are classic examples of a sans serif headline and serif body copy. But you can see above, left, that simply making the headline sans serif isn't quite enough. On the right, I used the same sans serif but made it bigger and bolder which multiplied the contrasts, making it stronger and more effective.

ROSEMARY
Faithfulness and remembrance.
PANSIES
Thoughts and love's wounds.
FENNEL
Flattery and sorrow.
COLUMBINE
Ingratitude and forsaken lovers.
RUE
Repentance, pity, grace, and forgiveness.
VIOLETS
Death, especially early death.

Rosemary
Faithfulness and remembrance.
Pansies
Thoughts and love's wounds.
Fennel
Flattery and sorrow.
Columbine
Ingratitude and forsaken lovers.
Rue
Repentance, pity, grace, and forgiveness.
Violets
Death, especially early death.

This is a goodhearted attempt to make a list easier to read by putting the headings in caps. But the contrast isn't quite enough.

This list communicates more clearly because of the contrast that allows your eyes to skim the heads. I also used extra "paragraph space above" each heading, as explained in Chapter 14, to more clearly separate each element. And I used lowercase instead of caps for the headings so they would be easier to read quickly.

Combining typefaces is one of the most satisfying aspects of design. If you find this intriguing and want to know more, read *The Non-Designer's Design Book;* the second half focuses on this particular challenge.

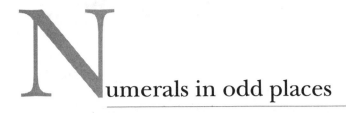

Numerals in odd places

Regarding superscripts, subscripts, and fractions.

Superscript and subscript

Don't forget about the superscript and subscript options. The superscript reduces the size of the selected text and *raises it up;* the subscript reduces the size of the text and *lowers it.*

You'll find the command for these options in your type styles menu.

- To create a superscript such as the **th** in **4th**, simply do this: type **4th**; select the **th** and choose "superscript."

- To create a subscript such as the **2** in H_2O, simply do this: type **H2O**; select the **2** and choose "subscript."

Page layout applications will allow you to determine exactly how small a super- or subscript character is, and how far it sits above or below the baseline (the invisible line on which type sits). Check the manual for your particular application.

If your application allows you to use a keyboard command shortcut for super- and subscripts, then use that shortcut *before* you type the character; then *after* you type it, *use the same keyboard shortcut* to return to normal type. For instance, if the keyboard shortcut is Command Shift + for superscript, you could type the following sequence to get **1st place:**

type **1**	then press Command Shift +
type **st**	then press Command Shift +
hit the *Spacebar*	then type **place**

Technically, the preferred form* of the ordinals "second" and "third" use just the "d," not "nd" or "rd." Thus the proper form is 2ᵈ and 3ᵈ, not 2ⁿᵈ or 3ʳᵈ. But you have to be brave to set it properly because most people will think you're doing it wrong, just like you have to be brave to properly pronounce your strong point as your "fort" (forte), not your "fortay," and to pronounce "victuals" as "vittles." Don't be a wimp.   *The Chicago Manual of Style, *8.4*

■

Fractions

Ever wonder where the fractions are? There aren't any. Well, that's not quite true—some fonts have at least three of the most common: ½, ¼, and ¾, but they are not readily available nor easily accessible. So most of the time you'll have to create your own. What you *don't* want is this kind of fraction: 2 3/8. You want this: 2⅜.

If you're writing a math book, you need to invest in a specialized font that carries all fractions. But for occasional use, try this technique:

1. Type the whole numeral and the fraction with no space between, like so: **21/2**

   Make sure to use the fraction bar (∕) instead of the slash (/). Press: **Shift Option 1**

2. Select the numeral **1** and make it a superscript (you'll find super- and subscript options in the type style menu; every program has them somewhere).

3. Select the numeral **2** and change its size to about half the point size of the original text.

4. It'll look like this: **2½**. Isn't that pretty?

You *could* apply the subscript style to the number on the bottom, *if* you use an application that allows you to adjust where the subscript sits. That is, you saw on the previous page that the default subscript makes a number drop below the baseline (the invisible line on which type sits). But some applications allow you to choose how far below the baseline the subscript sits—for fractions, it should sit at 0 (zero). Find that feature in your application, if it has one, and change the baseline position for subscripts to zero.

You can adjust the numbers around the fraction bar by kerning (see Chapter 9), if your application has a kerning feature.

Miscellaneous

Just a few asides that are important but don't rate their own little chapters.

- **Use italic and bold sparingly**—as you would a rich dessert. They're fine occasionally, but easy to overdose on. And they are not as easy to read as regular text, so you don't ever want to set large amounts of body copy in italic or bold.

- The standard format for A.M. and P.M. is **small caps.** Small caps are capital letters that are the same size as or not much bigger than lowercase: THESE ARE SMALL CAPS.

  There are no small caps on a typewriter so we were taught to type A.M. and P.M. in all caps. When set in all caps, though, the letters are very large and attach too much importance to themselves. Most applications on your Mac provide the option to set them properly: type the letters in *lowercase;* select them; choose "Small Caps" from your style menu. There should be a space after the number and periods after the letters: 8:30 A.M.

- Regarding **punctuation and parentheses,** the sentence punctuation goes *after* the closing parenthesis *if* what is inside the parentheses is *part of the main sentence* (as this phrase here). That goes for commas, semicolons, colons, and question marks as well.

  If what is inside the parentheses is *an entire statement of its own,* the ending punctuation belongs inside also, as in the following example. (If you set a complete and separate sentence inside the parentheses, the sentence begins with a capital letter and ends with its appropriate punctuation.)

∎

- When placing more than one column of text on a page, be sure to **align the first baselines of each column.** The *baseline* is the invisible line the type sits on, and when two bodies of text are next to each other, it is critical that the first lines across the columns align.

  Now, some designers are fussy about columns aligning their baselines all the way down the column. This is my general rule: *either* "hang the columns from the clothesline," meaning they are all aligned across the top; *or* "sit them on the ground," meaning they are aligned across the bottom of the page (or at least the bottoms of the columns are aligned). This works best when the columns are radically different heights—it does not work if they are all about the same height (if they are, it's usually best to hang them from the clothesline).

- Don't be afraid of "white space"! (It's called white, even if the paper is black; it refers to the space where there is no element printed on the page.) *The area on the page that does not have text or graphics on it is just as important as the area that does.* You may not be conscious of it yet, but your eyes are aware of it and how it's affecting everything else on the page.

  Don't be afraid to have wide margins, empty space before or after a major heading, a short bit of copy tucked up in the upper-left instead of spread out in the middle of the page. That's one of the greatest differences between a clean, professional, sophisticated look and an amateur look—the professional is not afraid to leave plenty of white space! It's okay to have empty space on the page.

- If you have to place text inside a box (which in general you should avoid), don't crowd it. Leave plenty of room on all sides. Generally the ideal is to have the same amount of space on all four sides, visually. If you are leaving more space on one or two sides intentionally, then make it obvious.

> This text is crowded, making it unappealing to read. The reader feels as cramped as the text.

> This text has more breathing space, thus appearing much more readable and inviting.

> I *want* more space on the bottom of this particular layout.

- When **typing numerals,** never use the lowercase L (l) for the number one (1), nor the capital letter O for a zero (0). Besides the fact that they have different shapes, the Mac reacts to them differently; if you'll be doing any sort of calculating or trying to enter a password or serial number, your computer will get very confused if an L is found in a list of numerals.

- Make a conscious effort to **be consistent.** If a heading is aligned left, then align left all the headings. If a heading is 18-point bold, then make all the headings 18-point bold. If a page number is on the lower, outer margin, they should all be there. Etc., etc., etc. Look for consistency in tabs, indents, fonts, punctuation, alignments, margins on all sides, etc. Using **style sheets** will make this task infinitely easier; no one should ignore style sheets. Check the manual for your program and learn to use style sheets.

■ When listing items, as in a résumé or catalog, please don't use a hyphen or asterisk in front of each item. The hyphen and asterisk were fine on the typewriter when we had no other option, but now we can use the standard bullet • (Option 8), or any of a great variety of others: ☞, ✔, ✖, ①, ②, ③, ○, ❑, ❐, ❑, ◆, or ✎ from the font Zapf Dingbats. Or try the Wingdings font to get characters like ∞, ✧, ◐, ❑, ➜, ❁, ✿, ✪, ☒, or ☑.

– Rosemary
  Faithfulness and
  remembrance.
	❖ **Rosemary**
	  Faithfulness and
	  remembrance.

– Pansies
  Thoughts and love's
  wounds.
	❖ **Pansies**
	  Thoughts and love's
	  wounds.

– Fennel
  Flattery and sorrow.
	❖ **Fennel**
	  Flattery and sorrow.

– Columbine
  Ingratitude and
  forsaken lovers.
	❖ **Columbine**
	  Ingratitude and
	  forsaken lovers.

– Rue
  Repentance, pity, grace,
  and forgiveness.
	❖ **Rue**
	  Repentance, pity, grace,
	  and forgiveness.

– Violets
  Death, especially early
  death.
	❖ **Violets**
	  Death, especially early
	  death.

Of course I cheated a little here. Not only did I use more interesting bullets, but I added contrast in the weights of the font, plus a little extra space above each heading.

■ **Avoid abbreviations** whenever possible. Rarely is it necessary to abbreviate St. for Street or Dr. for Drive. In body text, avoid words like lbs. for pounds or oz. for ounces (something like an order form, of course, is different).

When possible, spell out the name of the state as well. If you are going to abbreviate it, then at least do it right: in professional-level printed work, states are all abbreviated with two capital letters and no periods. California should never be abbreviated as Ca, Ca., or Calif. (Newspaper style is different; if you're a journalist or you typeset a newspaper, follow the in-house guidelines and ignore me.)

- The **punctuation in large type,** such as headlines or pull quotes (like those shown below) often appears unnecessarily large, placing too much visual emphasis on itself. Commas, apostrophes, quotation marks, periods, etc., should all be reduced a point size or two.

"Everything must end; meanwhile we must amuse ourselves."

15-point text on auto leading; no adjustments made.

—*Voltaire*

"Everything must end; meanwhile we must amuse ourselves."

—*Voltaire*

15-point text on 13-point leading; 13-point period, quotation marks, and semicolon; punctuation hung and by-line aligned.

- When selecting a word to change into **italic,** be sure to select the space *before* the word as well as the word itself; *don't* select the space *after* the word. Italic fonts take up less space than roman (non-italic) fonts. This, in addition to the fact that the characters slant to the right, can sometimes create a distracting bit of extra space before the italic word unless you also italicize that space and thus make it smaller. Yes, it's subtle. I'm probably one of the few people in the world who even cares.

n the web

Typographic principles are a little different on the web.

All of the principles outlined in this little book apply to any type of printed page. But at this point in the medium of the World Wide Web, things are a little different. Below is a list of guidelines.

- **Readability:** I go much more into depth about readability in print in *The Non-Designer's Type Book,* but for now, just realize that shorter line lengths are easier to read on the web. "Shorter," that is, than you would use in most print jobs, and definitely shorter than the entire width of a web page.

- **Bold or italic:** Anything that makes type less easy to read on a *printed* page must be avoided even more stringently on a *web* page. Use bold sparingly, and use italic even more sparingly.

- **Sans serif fonts:** Because of the limited resolution of any monitor, sans serif fonts are actually easier to read on the screen than many serif faces, provided lines are short enough and paragraphs are not excessively lengthy.

- **Underlining:** If you underline text in print, you go to jail. But on the web, the underline is an important clue to a link. Some designers prefer to use a specific color for links and remove the underline; this *can* be done well, but most pages with this technique tend to be confusing because the visitor isn't sure what is a link and what isn't and so has to run the mouse all over the page checking to see what's what. If you choose to eliminate underlines, please be very careful with your color choices and uses to avoid confusing the visitor.

- **Apostrophes and quotation marks:** In the HTML default text on the page, it's possible to use true apostrophes and quotation marks. But there are some older browsers that can't read the code for those marks and so some users might see nasty code instead of a lovely curly quote. If you think most of your visitors live in places where they are using up-to-date hardware and software, go ahead and set true quotes in your body copy; if your web site market is international, it's best to just use the standard typewriter quotation marks.

  However, if you create **graphic** headlines or buttons, there is no reason to use typewriter marks! The graphic will appear on the page as an image, not HTML text, and the apostrophe or quotation marks will look just like you set them. Don't make your site look amateurish by using **'** in graphic text.

- **Accent marks, super- and subscripts, dashes, kerning:** Well, these and most other typographic niceties generally have to be ignored on web pages. Perhaps someday web pages will have the sophisticated type capabilities of print, but until then, enjoy not having to worry about it. Remember, though, any type that is set as a graphic can still use all the typographic savvy you've got.

- **Email:** I get a lot of email in which people apologize for not setting true apostrophes and quotes. Y'know what? It's okay. Let go. That's the fabulous thing about email—you can let go. Most email messages we never print; we just read them and toss. So don't bother—enjoy the freedom! *I* don't even use true quotes in email.

  Of course, if you are presenting a newsletter or a résumé through email, you need to be more careful and follow the rules so you present a professional appearance. But for 99 percent of your email messages, you can comfortably use typewriter apostrophes and quotation marks and not feel guilty.

Note: I use a lowercase "w" in "web" to be consistent with the use of other communication media such as radio, telephone, and television.

Quiz

See how much you've learned!

In the following text there are over a dozen mistakes that need editing. They may be typos, inconsistencies, bad line breaks, wrong hyphenations, widows, orphans, or any of the myriad items mentioned in this little book. See how many changes you can suggest to make the type more professional. A few suggestions are on the following pages.

The Solace of Tra-vel

To the untravelled, territory other than their own familiar heath is invariably *fascinating.* Next to *love*, it is the one thing which *solaces* and *delights.* Things new are too *important* to be neglected, and *mind*, which is a mere refection of *sensory impressions*, succumbs to the *flood* of objects. Thus lovers are *forgotten*, *sorrows* laid aside, *death* hidden from view. There is a *world* of accumulated feeling back of the trite dramatic *expression* -- "I am going *away*".

THEODORE DREISER

Sister Carrie

- *The line length is too short for justified text, creating terrible word and letter spacing.*
- *Too many words are italicized.*
- *The three sans serifs on one page create conflict.*
- *There is a lack of contrast or concord.*

Contrast of fonts between head and body copy is wimpy. Don't underline.

Headline needs kerning.

The Solace of Tra-vel

Wrong and bad line break.

Don't indent the first paragraph. "To" needs kerning.

To the untravelled, territory other than their own familiar heath is invariably *fascinating.* Next to *love,* it is the one thing which *solaces* and *delights.* Things new are too

Adjust linespace so it's consistent with others.

Too much space after the periods.

Wrong font.

important to be neglected, and *mind,* which is a mere *refection* of *sensory impressions,* succumbs to the *flood* of objects. Thus lovers are *forgotten, sorrows* laid aside, *death* hidden from view. There is a *world* of accu-mulated feeling back of the trite dra-

Typo.

Use a ligature.

Two hyphen-ations in a row.

Get rid of the widow.

Period belongs inside quote.

matic *expression* -- "I am going away".

Wrong quotation marks.

Use an em dash with no spaces on either side.

THEODORE DREISER

These two items need a stronger visual connection with each other; they are also too large for their purpose.

Sister Carrie

*Don't underline; besides, it is totally redundant to underline **and** italicize.*

Unnecessary to have this set in all caps; makes it too important in relation to the rest of text.

Possible alternatives

These are but two of a myriad of possibilities for setting this prose.

The Solace of Travel

To the untravelled, territory other than their own familiar heath is invariably fascinating. Next to love, it is the one thing which solaces and delights. Things new are too important to be neglected, and mind, which is a mere reflection of sensory impressions, succumbs to the flood of objects. Thus lovers are forgotten, sorrows laid aside, death hidden from view. There is a world of accumulated feeling back of the trite dramatic expression—"I am going away."

Theodore Dreiser
Sister Carrie

The Solace of Travel

To the untravelled, territory other than their own familiar heath is invariably fascinating. Next to love, it is the one thing which solaces and delights. Things new are too important to be neglected, and mind, which is a mere reflection of sensory impressions, succumbs to the flood of objects. Thus lovers are forgotten, sorrows laid aside, death hidden from view. There is a world of accumulated feeling back of the trite dramatic expression—"I am going away."

Theodore Dreiser
Sister Carrie

Appendix A

The following is a compendium of the rules established in this book. You might want to check through them each time you complete a publication.

- ☐ Use only one space between sentences.
- ☐ Use real quotation marks.
- ☐ Check the punctuation used with quote marks.
- ☐ Use real apostrophes.
- ☐ Make sure the apostrophes are where they belong.
- ☐ Use en and em dashes where appropriate.
- ☐ Use the special characters whenever necessary, including super- and subscript.
- ☐ Spend the time to create nice fractions.
- ☐ If a correctly spelled word needs an accent mark, use it.
- ☐ Don't underline.
- ☐ Never use all caps in body text; rarely use it in heads.
- ☐ Kern all headlines where necessary.
- ☐ Never use the Spacebar to align text.
- ☐ Use a one-em first-line indent on all indented paragraphs.
- ☐ Don't indent first paragraphs.
- ☐ Use a decimal or right-aligned tab for the numbers in numbered paragraphs.
- ☐ Leave no widows or orphans.
- ☐ Never have more than two hyphenations in a row.

■

- ☐ Avoid too many hyphenations in any paragraph.

- ☐ On every line of text in the document, check all line breaks carefully. Be sensible.

- ☐ Keep the line spacing consistent.

- ☐ Tighten up the leading in lines with all caps or with few ascenders and descenders.

- ☐ Adjust the spacing between paragraphs; rarely use a full line of space between paragraphs in body text.

- ☐ Either indent the first line of paragraphs or add extra space between them—not both.

- ☐ Never justify the text on a short line.

- ☐ Hang the punctuation off the aligned edge.

- ☐ Use serif type for body text unless you are going to compensate for the lower readability of sans serif.

- ☐ Never combine two serif fonts on one page.

- ☐ Rarely combine two sans serif fonts on one page.

- ☐ Never combine more than three typefaces on one page (unless you've studied typography). So the gist is: if you're going to use more than one face, use one serif, one sans serif, and maybe a script or decorative face.

- ☐ Use italic and bold sparingly.

- ☐ Use proper punctuation with parentheses.

- ☐ Align the first baselines of juxtaposed columns.

- ☐ Encourage white space.

- ☐ Don't crowd text inside a box—let it breathe.

- ☐ Be consistent.

- ☐ Use some sort of bullet when listing items, not a hyphen.

- ☐ Avoid abbreviations.

- ☐ Use small caps for A.M. and P.M.; space once after the number, and use periods.

- ☐ Reduce the size of the punctuation marks in headlines.

- ☐ Set the space *before* an italic word also in italic, but not the space after.

- ☐ Don't be a wimp.

Appendix B

The following is a list of the most often-used special characters and accent marks. On the following pages are the key combinations for just about every accent you might need.

"	Option [	opening double quote
"	Option Shift [	closing double quote
'	Option]	opening single quote
'	Option Shift]	closing single quote; apostrophe
–	Option Hyphen	en dash
—	Option Shift Hyphen	em dash
…	Option ;	ellipsis (this character can't be separated at the end of a line as three periods can)
•	Option 8	bullet (easy to remember as it's the asterisk key)
fi	Option Shift 5	ligature of f and i
fl	Option Shift 6	ligature of f and l
©	Option g	
TM	Option 2	
®	Option r	
°	Option Shift 8	degree symbol (e.g., 102°F)
¢	Option $	
€	Option Shift 2	Euro symbol
/	Option Shift 1 (one)	fraction bar (this doesn't descend below the line like the slash does)
¡	Option 1 (one)	
¿	Option Shift ?	
£	Option 3	
ç	Option c	
Ç	Option Shift c	

Remember, to set an accent mark over a letter, press the Option key and the letter, then press the letter you want under it (see page 29).

´	Option e	
`	Option ~	(upper-left or next to the Spacebar)
¨	Option u	
~	Option n	
^	Option i	

Tilde	Press	Let go, then press
˜	Option n	Spacebar
ã	Option n	a
Ã	Option n	Shift a
ñ	Option n	n
Ñ	Option n	Shift n
õ	Option n	o
Õ	Option n	Shift o

Dieresis	Press	Let go, then press
¨	Option u	Spacebar
ä	Option u	a
Ä	Option u	Shift a
ë	Option u	e
Ë	Option u	Shift e
ï	Option u	i
Ï	Option Shift f	
ö	Option u	o
Ö	Option u	Shift o
ü	Option u	u
Ü	Option u	Shift u
ÿ	Option u	y
`	Option Shift `	

(` is next to 1, or next to Spacebar;
the same key as the regular ˜key)

Circumflex	Press	Let go, then press
^	Option i	Spacebar
â	Option i	a
Â	Option Shift m	
ê	Option i	e
Ê	Option i	Shift e
î	Option i	i
Î	Option Shift d	
ô	Option i	o
Ô	Option Shift j	
û	Option i	u
Û	Option i	Shift u

■

Acute	Press	Let go, then press
´	Option e	Spacebar
á	Option e	a
Á	Option e or Option Shift y	Shift a
é	Option e	e
É	Option e	Shift e
í	Option e	i
Í	Option e or Option Shift s	Shift i
ó	Option e	o
Ó	Option e or Option Shift h	Shift o
ú	Option e	u
Ú	Option e or Option Shift ;	Shift u

Grave	Press	Let go, then press
`	Option ` (` is next to 1, or next to Spacebar; the same key as the regular ˜key)	Spacebar
à	Option `	a
À	Option `	Shift a
è	Option `	e
È	Option `	Shift e
ì	Option `	i
Ì	Option `	Shift i
ò	Option `	o
Ò	Option ` or Option Shift l (letter el)	Shift o
ù	Option `	u
Ù	Option `	Shift u

Miscellaneous	Press:
å	Option a
Å	Option Shift a
ç	Option c
Ç	Option Shift c

Index

Index

R

rag right margin, 50, 60
rant, 16
readability, 63–64
    example of good and not-so-good, 64
    on the web, 76
registered symbol, how to type it, 83
Returns, never hit two between paragraphs, 55–58
rivers in type, 59–60
rulers
    change to another measurement system, 60
    indent markers in, 38
    invisible defaults tabs in, 42
    set indents and outdents, 39
    tabs and indents in, 38–44
    tab markers in, 40
rule (line) under text, 31

S

sans serif type, 63–64
    don't combine them, 65
    good for web pages, 76
    make it more readable, 64
screenwriting, font for, 14
serial numbers, use the correct numerals, 73
serif type, 63–64
    combining two serif faces, 66
    what is serif type?, 63
Shakespeare, William
    As You Like It, 59
    Comedy of Errors, 55–58
    King Lear, 50
    Sonnet 3, 61–62
signage, legible typefaces for, 63–64
slash vs. fraction bar, 70
small caps for A.M. and P.M., 71
smart quotes, 16
Spacebar, don't use it to align text, 37
spaces, non-breaking, 62
spacing
    after punctuation, 13–14
    em space, indent for paragraphs, 57
    indent or space after paragraphs, not both, 58
    justified text, 59–60
    kerning, 35–36
    leading, 51–54
    letterspacing, 35–36
    line length, optimum measurement, 60
    linespacing, 51–54
      too much between lines of all caps, 54
    non-breaking spaces, 62
    paragraphs, between them, 55–58
    rivers in type, 59–60
    word spacing, justification causes inconsistent word spacing, 59
special characters, 25–28
    list, including accent marks, 83–85
    list of and how to type them, 28
style sheets for consistency, 73
superscript and subscript, 69
    in fractions, 70
symbols, 25–28
    lists of and how to type them, 28, 83

T

tabs and indents, 37–44
    em space, indent for paragraphs, 57
    indents
      first-line indent and outdent, 39
      first-line indent marker, 38
      indent left and right edges, how to, 38
      margins as opposed to indents, 37
      markers for, 38
    paragraphs
      don't indent the first one, 57
      how to type bulleted ones, 43
      to the Mac, 37
    rulers
      how to indent and outdent, 39
      importance of, 37
      indent markers in, 38
      move markers independently, 39
      tab markers in, 40
    tabs
      accumulation of tabs in a line, 42
      examples of, 40
      four different kinds and what they do, 40
      how to set and use them, the basics, 41
      invisible tabs, 42
      most important features of, 42
      numbered lists, 44
      practice exercise, 43
      where to find them, 41
Taylor, Laura Egley, photographs by, 72
temperature, apostrophe in, 20
tilde, how to type it, 84
Tollett, John, 4, 18
trademark symbol, how to type it, 83
typographer's quotes, 16

U

underlines
    options instead of underlining, 31–32
    web pages, underline is important, 76
    why not to use it in print, 31
unprofessional type, the most visible sign, 16

V

vittles, 69
Voltaire, 74

W

Wingdings for bullets, 74
web, lowercase "w" for web, 77
web pages, typography on, 76–77
white space, it's okay, 72
widows, 45
Wilde, Oscar, 50
wimp, don't be one, 67, 82
Word, Microsoft, tabs, where to find them, 41
word spacing
    line length, optimum measurement, 60

Z

Zapf Dingbats for bullets, 74

Colophon: This book was produced in Adobe InDesign. The main type families are ITC New Baskerville and ITC **Bailey Sans.**

88